IMAGES
of America

CHICAGO'S
50 YEARS OF POWWOWS

IMAGES of America
CHICAGO'S 50 YEARS OF POWWOWS

American Indian Center of Chicago

Nora Lloyd, Warren Perlstein, Joseph Podlasek, David Spencer
In collaboration with
Jane Stevens
Illinois State Museum

Copyright © 2004 by American Indian Center of Chicago

ISBN 978-153-1618-711

Published by Arcadia Publishing
Charleston SC, Chicago IL, Portsmouth NH, San Francisco CA

Library of Congress Catalog Card Number: 2004106923

For all general information contact Arcadia Publishing at:
Telephone 843-853-2070
Fax 843-853-0044
E-mail sales@arcadiapublishing.com
For customer service and orders:
Toll-Free 1-888-313-2665

Visit us on the internet at http://www.arcadiapublishing.com

This book is dedicated to the greater Native American community of Chicago—past, present, and future.

CONTENTS

Acknowledgments		6
Foreword, by Joseph Podlasek, Executive Director, AIC		7
Introduction: What is a Powwow?		11
1.	The Four Circles of Powwow	13
2.	The First Circle: The Drum is the Heart	15
3.	The Second Circle: The Men at the Drum	19
4.	The Third Circle: Songbirds	25
5.	Community Creates the Fourth Circle	31
6.	Specials and Vendors	99
7.	Next Generation	115
8.	50 Years of Powwow: The Exhibition of Storytelling	125
The Newberry Library's D'Arcy McNickle Center		
	for American Indian History, by Brian Hosmer, Director	140
American Indian Center of Chicago		143

ACKNOWLEDGMENTS

Special thanks to Ben Bearskin Sr., Nancy Bechtol, Sterling Big Bear Jr., Orlando Cabanban, Armand Esai, Nizhoni Hodge, Joe Kazumura, Nora Lloyd, Clovia Malatare, Alice Murata, Shann Maupin, Beverly Moeser, Jan Newman, Mary Petracek, Warren Perlstein, Susan Power, Christine Redcloud, Norma Robertson, R.J. Smith, E. Donald Two-Rivers, Robert Wapahi, Peter F. Weil, Leroy Wesaw, Hilda Williams, and AIC Board of Directors, staff, and all other community members who have helped throughout the year.

Exhibition Committee:
Nora Lloyd
Warren Perlstein
Joseph Podlasek
David Spencer
Jane Stevens

The American Indian Center of Chicago acknowledges the support and assistance of many organizations and individuals that helped make this book possible. Special thanks to The Newberry Library's D'Arcy McNickle Center for American Indian History, Illinois State Museum sites, Chicago Historical Society, The Field Museum of Natural History, Spurlock Museum at the University of Illinois, Urbana-Champaign, The Illinois Arts Council, Illinois Humanities Council, Department of Cultural Affairs, City of Chicago, City Arts II, and The Rockefeller Foundation Fellowship in the Humanities.

Foreword

Boozhoo. This book has been a long time coming from the American Indian Center of Chicago. It is a tribute to the oldest urban Indian center in the country, established during the 1950s Relocation Program. We are very proud and honored to share our 50 Years of Powwow photographs for educational and historical documentation.

Thanks to the many community members, past and present, and friends of the American Indian Center, we have assembled a small but wonderful collection of photographs. These images span 50 years of traditions being passed from generation to generation within an urban setting and represent one of the most important parts of the American Indian culture in Chicago—the powwow.

It is an honor and privilege to have worked on this book with many elders, community members, organizations, and this committee. Just like our entire community does daily, this committee provided countless hours of volunteer work to see our community share our proud culture in a positive way.

Our community has been stereotyped in many ways over the years. Publishing *Chicago's 50 Years of Powwows* is a great opportunity to educate many people and express a "first voice" perspective and define the positive roles that instill pride and self-respect in our children's lives. Powwow is only one part of a much larger and beautiful culture. Not all American Indians celebrate through powwows, nor is it the only way we celebrate our culture. But it is a very important part of our day to day lives. We are a proud community that lives by our beliefs and traditions.

The written information in this book is based on stories and traditions shared by elders in the Chicago setting. We can not present all the complexities of Native American culture in this book. We would, however, like to encourage everyone to come and learn more at the American Indian Center and our Annual November Powwow. If you are not in Chicago, please look up an American Indian Center in your part of the country. They will be happy to help too.

For our future generations and the education of all people, I hope you enjoy this book as we continue to expand your minds and lives. *Mii gwetch.*

—Joseph Podlasek, Executive Director, American Indian Center

AMERICAN INDIAN CENTER, 2003.

MISSION STATEMENT
"To promote the fellowship among Indian people of all Tribes living in metropolitan Chicago, and to create bonds of understanding and communications between Indians and non-Indians in this city. To advance the general welfare of American Indians into the metropolitan community life; to foster the economic and educational advancement of Indian people, to sustain cultural, artistic, and avocational pursuits; and to perpetuate Indian cultural values."

VISION STATEMENT
"We envision the American Indian Center as the authentic primary resource for urban American Indian culture, and a welcoming home for all American Indians."

American Indian Center of Chicago
1630 W. Wilson Ave.
Chicago, IL 60640
www.aic-chicago.org
773-275-5871

Winnebago Color Guard, Chief Ben Winneshiek (right), American Indian Center's Annual Powwow, Navy Pier Ballroom, c. 1987.

ANGIE DECORAH, JOSEPHINE FOX, CLIFFORD BLACKBIRD, AND SUSAN POWER AT THE 50TH ANNUAL AIC POWWOW, UNIVERSITY OF ILLINOIS AT CHICAGO, 2003.

Introduction
WHAT IS A POWWOW?

The powwow is at once a celebration and extension of Indian traditions through the arts (visual and performance) and a critical vehicle for transmitting those traditions to our younger generation. Although traditional aspects of Native American culture have evolved and are still practiced in urban centers, it is conveyed that respective Indian Nations who reside in Chicago culturally exchange among themselves through powwow culture. Powwows are places and times to rekindle old friendships, reaffirm traditional values, share, and introduce the vivid and vital spectacle of contemporary Indian culture to the larger Chicago community.

The Annual American Indian Center of Chicago Powwow, held each November, is the largest form of American Indian artistic and cultural education activity, providing a platform for self-representation through traditional and contemporary Native art forms. It has become an indispensable and defining cultural endeavor in Indian Chicago.

Historically, powwows evolved from ceremonials of the Grass Dance Societies that formed during the early 1800s. Over a period of time, Indian relations with the government translated to ceasing a myriad of tribal customs and religious practices. However, the Grass Dance was one of the few celebrations allowed into this new era. As other communities and tribes were invited to these celebrations, rights of ownership of sacred items of the Grass Dance were transferred from one tribe to another. Intertribalism commenced with the sharing of these songs and dances.

In the 1920s, some powwows became "intertribal" meaning that they were open for all tribes to attend, and these events happened sporadically. World War II brought a revival to the powwow world, and since then powwows have been growing, changing, and adapting to modern ways, while retaining their cultural roots. Brighter colors, modern conveniences to short cut regalia making, more athletic and trained motions, and even a new style of dance has emerged with the passage of time.

There are several different kinds of powwows (e.g. memorials, birthdays, fundraisers, etc.), however, the two most common are known as traditional and competition powwows. Traditional powwows are executed for purposes of honor in traditions; retaining and celebrating Native values. Traditional powwows are informal, and include ceremonies such as giveaways (gifts for those who have helped the inspired gift giver) or "first" dances (support-based ceremony, inviting and celebrating the first dance of an individual into the dance circle). On the other hand, while traditional values are not absent, a competition powwow is held in a festival environment. The competition powwow provides an opportunity for both Native and non-Native persons to learn about Native American culture, including but not limited to the wide spectrum of traditional Indian art and music. Spectators enjoy contemporary Native American cuisine (diverse foods from respective Tribal Nations), purchase various art items and thematic Native products, and watch dancers and singers compete for the right to be named champion. Significant prize money is involved with competition powwows. It is important to note that most of the consecrated ceremonies are no longer part of the powwow (e.g. naming ceremonies are now conducted in the privacy of the family), but honoring ceremonies remain today.

In Chicago, powwow is produced for artistic expression, cultural exchange, celebration, and educational endeavors. Additionally, powwow reinforces the presence of Native Americans and their contributions to the cultural fabric of the City of Chicago and the State of Illinois.

The photographs in this book document a half century of the powwow experience.

THE FOUR CIRCLES OF POWWOW, AIC ANNUAL POWWOW, NORTHEASTERN ILLINOIS UNIVERSITY, 2002.

One
THE FOUR CIRCLES OF POWWOW

A powwow consists of four circles. The Drum is at the center of the powwow, forming the first circle. Surrounding the Drum is a ring of men singers; the second circle. Women singers support the men; they are the third circle. The fourth circle embraces everyone else at the powwow: the dancers, community members, and visitors.

OVERVIEW OF DRUM AND DANCE ARENA, UNIVERSITY OF ILLINOIS AT CHICAGO, 2003.

Two
THE FIRST CIRCLE
THE DRUM IS THE HEART

The most essential part of any powwow is the Drum. The Drum is highly revered and is known as "Grandfather."

Grandfather is a link to the past, an elder, a teacher who provides guidance, lessons, and makes communication to the past possible. Contextualizing Grandfather as an instrument is wrong because he is a living element. He gives us the heartbeat. Grandfather is not the creator but the sustainer of life for the people, Grandfather has his own creation story.

It is believed that Grandfather came from woman. Woman is the closest physical element to the Creator because she is a life-giver as well. Over time, woman then gave Grandfather to man to provide needed protection. Thus, the male is the protector while woman remains the nurturer. This is an oral lesson which is still practiced and taught today.

If one views the Drum through a popular lens, the Drum then becomes an object built from material and simply viewed as a tool for performance. In contrast, when Grandfather is viewed through the Native perspective, Grandfather is honored as life and its function is a connection to the past.

Grandfather as an object is created with elements of life. Our four-legged brothers spend a short time in the physical world because that is their purpose—to sacrifice their lives to sustain the heartbeat of the people. Grandfather is able to possess skin, and a skeleton made of our cousin the tree of life.

Therefore, Grandfather is life. Grandfather possesses medicine. Grandfather is a person of different form. Grandfather is our relation, an immediate family member.

Singers Place Tobacco on the Drum and Offer a Prayer to Grandfather.

Drum and Dancers at NAES (Native American Educational Services) Powwow, Mather Park, 2003.

DRUM ON EXHIBIT, 2003. While not in use the Drum is on its side.

Three
THE SECOND CIRCLE
THE MEN AT THE DRUM

*Singers offer tobacco to Grandfather, the heartbeat and circles form,
the powwow can now begin. . . .*

The Drum (a powwow term that conveys the group of singers) is at the center of the arena and the center of attention. The big powwow Drum is made from a wooden (or sometimes metal) shell covered in rawhide. Today, cowhide is common, although buffalo, horse, steer, or moose hide is sometimes used. The sticks used to strike the Drum are usually thin fiberglass rods with a leather handle and leather padded head. There are about ten people on an average Drum; seven or eight men and two or three women. The singers on a Drum are required to know a variety of songs because they are expected to be able to sing for an entire powwow without repeating a song.

Songs are composed for many reasons and exist for the people. Songs from Indian country, have a direct relation to the oral tradition. These songs have power and when sung "in a good way" we allow the environment an opportunity to receive the good. The environment (the land and the people who derive from it) is the ultimate receiver of the good. Without the land where would we be?

In Native America, songs are composed and sung at ceremonies (e.g. healing, prayer, Stomp dances, sweat lodge, pipe, etc.), powwows, wakes and funerals, veteran gatherings, birthdays, weddings—basically at any social event. There are literally tens of thousands of songs that are hundreds of years old and are still sung today (this number is purely estimated when considering the oral history of Native America as opposed to written history).

ARLIS WHITEMAN RUNS HIM (CENTERMOST), CROW AGENCY DRUM, THE CHICAGO AVENUE ARMORY, 1960.

JAMES KLEIN, ALAN MANITOWABI, GERALD CLEVELAND, NAVY PIER BALLROOM, 1973.

Archie Black Owl Holding Baby, Waters' Family Drum, 1958.

Today, there are two kinds of songs, word songs and vocable songs. Word songs are generally the older songs because Native languages were widely spoken. On the other hand, vocable songs are composed regularly due to the growing absence of language and the formation of intertribal communities. Vocables are melodic sounds used in place of language and words. It is an honor to sit at the Drum. Drum is medicine. The Drum provides balance; a process of healing "for all living things," for the good of all people and the land from which we came. Most powwows share a commonality in regard to the collection of songs performed:

Flag Song
Just as the United States has its national anthem, almost every tribal nation has its own flag song, which is sung after the Grand Entry. The flag song is sung to honor the Eagle Feather Staff and respective colors and should be recognized with proper respect.

Contest Songs
Contest songs are composed to test the dancers' skill. They often speed up or suddenly stop at unexpected times in order for judges to determine the champion dancer. Contest songs are usually written for a particular dance style, such as Fancy, Grass, or Jingle Dress.

Sizzortail Singers, University of Illinois at Chicago, 2000.

Northern Style Singers, c. 1970s.

SHKI BMAADZI (*Ojibwe*: NEW LIFE, NEW BEGINNINGS) SINGERS AT THE CHICAGO HISTORICAL SOCIETY, 1998.

INTERTRIBAL
The most common form of song is the intertribal or friendship song. Everyone is to dance to these songs. Intertribal songs are performed throughout the duration of the powwow to get everyone on their feet and dancing.

VETERAN SONGS
Songs have been written for veterans of World War I, World War II, Korea, Vietnam, and Desert Storm. Respective tribal nations have their own veteran songs. When a veteran song is sung, it is customary to stand and men remove their hats in reverence for those who served their country.

TWO STEP (OR RABBIT DANCE) SONGS
This is one of the few dances where men and women dance as partners. Women choose their partners. Couples, holding hands, circle the Drum and follow the lead of the head dancers.

QUITTING (OR TRAVELING) SONGS
It is custom at the end of a powwow to close the dance with a quitting song. Quitting or traveling songs are sung to ensure everyone safe travel home.

A Chicago community elder says, "Sing these songs in a good way . . . always sing them to the best of your ability because the people are listening."

SMOKEYTOWN SINGERS, NORTHEASTERN ILLINOIS UNIVERSITY, 2002.

WISCONSIN DELLS SINGERS, UNIVERSITY OF ILLINOIS AT CHICAGO, 2003.

Four
THE THIRD CIRCLE
SONGBIRDS

In powwow country, women singers are known as canaries. Women's voices fuse with the men's voices to form beautiful harmonies, instilling strength and pride in our children and honoring those who came before us.

Oral histories articulate stories of the prominent role of women in Native communities. As Native societies evolve and transform, traditional practices become affected, resulting in a contemporary practice of mistranslations, or remnants combined with modern philosophies. Nonetheless, long ago women warrior societies of singers existed. Although songs from these societies were not "powwow" songs, they were vital to the daily lives of Native people as they celebrated life-giving and renewal.

Songs are composed for many purposes. Women continue to perform for specific occasions including: songs for delivering babies, for childless women to have children, lullabies, food gathering and preparation, songs that are connected to making utilitarian necessities (i.e. clothing, pots, tools, etc), as medicine for female illnesses, mourning or burial songs, and animal songs related to medicine or story songs.

In the days of the modern powwow, what hasn't changed is the call of the woman warrior—the "lu-lu" (shrill or high-pitched ululation). As the third circle provides beauty and balance into powwow songs, it is equally wonderful to experience the high praise of the woman's lu-lu. The lu-lu signifies an appreciation of an honoring song or dance. It is a sound associated with both mourning and celebration.

In Chicago, a continual practice of elder-to-youth or cultural bearer-to-youth learning is common. The importance of the third circle is recognized as women hold a position of respect. One story explains that woman is closer to the Creator as she also is a life-giver. Therefore, it is the responsibility of the second circle to protect the heartbeat while the third circle nurtures the heartbeat.

The role of women has changed in tribal societies since Western contact. In our tribal nations, women have remained strong, vital parts of society, existing in harmony with men. Fortunately, because of our connection and honor to those who came before, women remain the epitome of Native survival. Still today women warriors seek to create healthy communities and mend the circles in our lives and the lives of others around us. These warriors are mothers, daughters, sisters, grandmothers, and wives. They are also honored and respected healers, educators, students, artists, activists, scientists, and dancers.

Women Singers, American Indian Center, 1987.

Women Singers, University of Illinois at Chicago, 2003.

Norma Robertson (left) and Christine Redcloud (right), Chicago Historical Society, 1998.

ANTONIA SHEEHY (LEFT) AND CLOVIA MALATARE (RIGHT), UNIVERSITY OF ILLINOIS AT CHICAGO, 2003.

FROM LEFT TO RIGHT, CHRISTINE REDCLOUD, MAVIS NECONISH, NICOLE DALL, AND RAEANNE HIDALGO, NORTHEASTERN ILLINOIS UNIVERSITY, 2002.

Honorary Veteran Ron Jourdan (left) and Head Veteran George Martin, University of Illinois at Chicago, 2003.

Powwows are an important part of Indian peoples' lives. Although many tribal nations don't have a powwow culture in their traditional practices, in today's era, powwows provide an environment, and more importantly, a "circle" to represent the cycle of life. Powwows are not only a culturally educational endeavor, they also provide a time for members of the Chicago Indian community and the larger community to come together to celebrate and promote Indian pride and intertribal unity in this massive urban center. The powwow circle brings people closer together; closer to their family, friends, and to their Native culture.

Five
COMMUNITY CREATES THE FOURTH CIRCLE

THE POWWOW OPENS WITH THE GRAND ENTRY
What begins as a trickle turns into a cascade, as powwow participants flood the fourth circle. Veterans and flag-bearers lead the procession, followed by Powwow "royalty" who represent various Native American communities, culminating with dignitaries and dancers. The Grand Entry song is followed by a flag song, then an invocation to bless the gathering.

HONORING THE VETERANS
American Indian veterans are seen as warriors and protectors of the people. As such, they hold an honored place at the powwow and lead the Grand Entry procession.

A necessary part of any powwow is the recognition of U.S. veterans. Today's veterans are honored and respected as warriors who have met the challenges of life and death in defense of the "The People." At powwows, veterans are asked to be flag bearers and to commence the start of the powwow celebration. The colors are very important to the Native Americans, further recognizing the flag of the United States and Canada. Also, the eagle feather staff and a flag for each branch of the military are carried into the dance circle and posted. The eagle staff, comprised of multiple eagle feathers, serves as the flag for Native Americans, inclusively. Other respected individuals include princesses from visiting tribes and organizations.

VETERAN WITH FLAG, UNIVERSITY OF ILLINOIS AT CHICAGO, 2003.

Indian people have many ways of honoring their veterans, especially their wounded veterans and the ones who have not returned to their loved ones. At every powwow there are honoring dances and songs. It is a part of Indian tradition to take time to show honor and respect for those who have met the challenges of life and death in defense of the people.

In a modern society that often doesn't seem to pay much attention to veterans, the honor accorded to veterans at the powwow can seem surprising to someone not familiar with Indian culture and customs. Veterans are asked to be flag bearers, called upon to retrieve dropped eagle feathers and honored in a multitude of veteran songs. The respect shown to veterans is an integral part of American Indian cultures, a tradition from times when the welfare of every village depended on the number and ability of its fighting men. To be a warrior was a man's purpose in life and the most honorable death a man could have was to fall defending the people. To the Indian people, the well-being of the entire tribe was more important than that of any individual; and so the warriors were honored because they were willing to give their lives in order that the people might live.

Today's veterans are accorded the same tokens of honor and respect as the warriors of times past, and, in many tribes, bravery is still revered as one of the four virtues: bravery, generosity, wisdom, and fortitude.

COLOR GUARD, UNIVERSITY OF
ILLINOIS AT CHICAGO, 2003.

VETERANS WITH EAGLE STAFFS AND FLAGS, UNIVERSITY OF ILLINOIS AT CHICAGO, 2003.

Pat and Herman Logan, Head Dancers, University of Illinois at Chicago, 2001.

Head Staff

It is imperative to select and invite qualified knowledgeable and experienced individuals to serve as "head staff," (head dancers, head veteran dancer, arena director, and the emcee). The leadership of the head male and female dancer is vital and their knowledge of the complex powwow dance culture deems respect by their peers and younger dancers. The head veteran (combat veteran) serves as the overall leader of the powwow circle. The head veteran carries the responsibilities of protecting and being caretaker of the eagle feather staff. The position and responsibility of the emcee mandates a wealth of powwow knowledge. The emcee informs and educates the audience on specific Native traditions and powwow culture. The arena director is the powwow's conductor, responsible for the overall powwow organization, providing guidance for the dancers, and coordination for the Drums and singers, making the powwow form a smooth transition from one event to another.

LEONARD MALATARE, EMCEE, NAES COLLEGE ANNUAL POWWOW, MATHER PARK, 2001.

ROBERT "BOBBO" SMITH, ARENA DIRECTOR, UNIVERSITY OF ILLINOIS AT CHICAGO, 2001.

LANA KING, MISS INDIAN CHICAGO, NAVY PIER BALLROOM, 1985.

POWWOW ROYALTY
Chicago's Native American princesses are ambassadors who travel across the country to other powwows, representing their tribe(s) and community. Princesses are elected annually by community consensus. They are given sashes that bear their name and their organization's name, as well as a beautifully beaded crown to exhibit their royalty. In Chicago, the American Indian Center sponsors three princesses; Little Miss Indian Chicago, Junior Miss Indian Chicago, and Miss Indian Chicago.

CROWNING OF AIC ROYALTY, UNIVERSITY OF ILLINOIS AT CHICAGO, 2003.

AUTUMN ROSE BIG BEAR, LITTLE MISS INDIAN CHICAGO, 2002–2003, UNIVERSITY OF ILLINOIS AT CHICAGO, 2003.

FROM LEFT TO RIGHT: SARAH J. KEAHNA, JOANN MANEY, AND MAYOR RICHARD M. DALEY CROWNING LITTLE MISS INDIAN CHICAGO, c. 1980s.

ARISSA YOLANDA ST. GERMAINE, JUNIOR MISS INDIAN CHICAGO SHAKING HANDS, UNIVERSITY OF ILLINOIS AT CHICAGO, 2003.

AIC ROYALTY 2003–2004, LINDA MARIE WHITE, MISS INDIAN CHICAGO (LEFT) AND WYNONA LYNN DEON, JUNIOR MISS INDIAN CHICAGO (RIGHT), UNIVERSITY OF ILLINOIS AT CHICAGO, 2003.

LANA KING, MISS INDIAN CHICAGO, NAVY PIER BALLROOM, 1985.

ANGEL STARR (RIGHT), GRAND ENTRY, UNIVERSITY OF ILLINOIS AT CHICAGO, 2003.

GRAND ENTRY, UNIVERSITY OF ILLINOIS AT CHICAGO, 2003.

GRAND ENTRY, UNIVERSITY OF ILLINOIS AT CHICAGO, 2001.

Every dance tells a story . . . each dance has its own regalia . . .

Most competition powwows are similar, as they offer competitive dancing and singing. However the complexities of powwows occur in dance styles and regalia. Every dancer has his or her own particular style. Members of diverse tribal nations dance in traditional powwow regalia (often referred to as "costume" and this term is inaccurate). Regalia design and color schemes signify special events, honor a person's life, convey traditions or legends, and exhibit familial ties to tribal affiliation and clans. The following pages offer a breakdown of dances, regalia, and stories of origin.

LOUIS DELGADO, AMERICAN INDIAN CENTER, 1985.

HERMAN LOGAN (LEFT) AND GERALD CLEVELAND (RIGHT), UNIVERSITY OF ILLINOIS AT CHICAGO, 2003.

Jaime Begay (left), Grand Entry, University of Illinois at Chicago, 2003.

KEN FUNMAKER, SR., NAVY PIER BALLROOM, 1985.

MEN'S TRADITIONAL DANCE
Every dance at the powwow tells a story, and often there are different versions of each story. According to some storytellers, the Men's Traditional Dance recounts the exploits and bravery of warriors in battle. Others tell of a hunter's skill; his movements are akin to stalking an animal. The regalia of a Traditional Dancer pays honor to the animal spirits, especially eagles and hawks. His attire consists of eagle feather bustles, a bone bead breastplate, leggings, beaded moccasins, a beaded belt, ankle bells, a porcupine roach headdress, breechcloth, various beaded accessories, and he carries an eagle feather fan.

Pete Moore (left), Traditional Dancers, Navy Pier Ballroom, c. 1985.

Dennis White, University of Illinois at Chicago, 2003.

TRADITIONAL DANCERS, NAVY PIER BALLROOM, 1986.

PATRICK TAHAWAH, 1975

Gabe Cleveland, Navy Pier Ballroom, 1985.

Traditional Dancers, Northeastern Illinois University, 2002.

DALE ROBERTS (CENTER), NORTHEASTERN ILLINOIS UNIVERSITY, 2002.

MEN'S GRASS DANCE
Of the many stories about the Grass Dance, perhaps the most well-known is that Grass Dancer created a dance circle by stomping down the tall prairie grasses. Modern powwows often begin with a single Grass Dancer who ceremonially prepares the dance area for all the other participants.

CHAYAN ALMOS MAHKIMETAS, UNIVERSITY OF ILLINOIS AT CHICAGO, 2003.

SATEKO DANFORTH, NORTHEASTERN ILLINOIS UNIVERSITY, 2002.

A great deal has been written about the Grass or "Omaha" Dance, one of the oldest of the surviving tribal dances. Borrowed from the Omaha tribe, perhaps in the 1860s, the Grass Dance is very popular today. Dancers' outfits are decorated with thick hanks of long, colorful fringes, which sway gracefully with the movement of the dancers' bodies in a movement reminiscent of the long blowing grass of the prairie. Several tribes dance their own version of the dance, and some say that the fringes replace the grasses that the dancers originally would tuck into their belts. Another tribe remembers dancing in order to flatten out the long prairie grasses in preparation for a ceremony. Still others think it originated to celebrate victory over an enemy. Many dancers wear the hair roach, the crow belt, and the eagle-bone whistle—originally emblems of the Omaha Society.

GRASS DANCERS, NORTHEASTERN ILLINOIS UNIVERSITY, 2002.

The basic step of the Omaha dance involves the ball of one foot being tapped on the "one beat" and placed down flatly with the next beat, then repeating the action on the opposite foot without missing a beat. Each time the foot is placed flatly on the ground, the weight shifts to that foot. Dancers are expected to keep their heads moving either up and down with the beat of the Drum, nodding quickly several times to each beat, or moving from side to side. The purpose of this movement is to keep the roach crest feathers spinning. To keep the feathers moving constantly is one sign of a good dancer.

BOYE LADD, UNIVERSITY OF ILLINOIS AT CHICAGO, 2000.

MEN'S FANCY DANCE
This contemporary dance originated in Oklahoma. A difficult dance to perform, it requires strength, agility, and endurance. Some stories describe the men's fancy dance as a preparation for war.

Dancers wear a modern dance outfit with its roots in the old grass dance. It is a relatively new dance style. The dancers wear two brilliantly colored feather bustles, and their outfits are much flashier and more brightly colored than the men's traditional outfits.

The Fancy Dance, performed mostly by boys and young men, is based on the standard "double step" of the Men's Traditional and Grass Dances, but it takes off from there with highly elaborate dance footwork, greatly increased speed, acrobatic steps and motions and more varied body movements. The Fancy Dance is a freestyle kind of dance, in which dancers do whatever they can, as long as they keep up with the music. As in other dance styles, the dancers must follow the changing beat of the Drum and stop when the music stops, with both feet on the ground. This dance is a modern expression of Indian people combining the pace of today with the traditions of yesterday.

Sonny Boy Starr, University of Illinois at Chicago, 2003.

Daryl Jack, University of Illinois at Chicago, 2003.

ERIC LOGAN, 1973.

Some parts of the Fancy Dancer's regalia are:

Hair Roach: an item worn on the head of most dancers, usually made of deer tail hair and porcupine hair guard.

Bells: (sheep or sleigh) help to maintain the rhythm of the dance.

Bustles: these are the arrangement of feathers worn on the neck and back of fancy dancers. The primary part of the bustle is the feather. These were at one time, eagle feathers. Today, many are made of white or dark turkey feathers decorated with small colorful feathers called hackles. In addition to the bustles of the Fancy Dancers, another noticeable part is the elaborate beadwork. Many dancers strive to have all matching beadwork.

Windy White and Bobby Bird, Navy Pier Ballroom, 1986.

Windy White, Navy Pier Ballroom, 1986.

EDITH JOHNS, c. 1985.

WOMEN'S TRADITIONAL DANCE
Depending on the individual's tribe, this dance includes more than one dance style. In this dance, women wear either buckskin or cloth regalia. Both styles carry a shawl folded over an arm, and carry an eagle feather fan. Additionally, outfits vary according to tribal background. The Women's Traditional Dance is one that requires much skill to stay in perfect rhythm; stepping lightly, slightly 'bobbing' up and down, and allowing the fringe on their dresses and shawls to sway gracefully.

Pearl Reed, Navy Pier Ballroom, 1986.

VANNY WHEELOCK, TRADITIONAL DANCER, NAES COLLEGE POWWOW, MATHER PARK, 2002.

The patterns and designs of a dancer's regalia are often handed down from mother to daughter and nearly every aspect of an outfit is handmade and hand-sewn. Many times the entire top of the dance dress is beaded with symbolic designs that hold meaning to the individual owner. The dress may also be adorned with ribbon work, elks' teeth and shells. Accessories include decorated moccasins, knee-high leggings, beaded or concho belts, hair earrings, chokers, and necklaces.

WOMEN'S TRADITIONAL DANCERS, GRAND ENTRY, UNIVERSITY OF ILLINOIS AT CHICAGO, 2003.

WOMEN'S TRADITIONAL DANCERS, GRAND ENTRY, UNIVERSITY OF ILLINOIS AT CHICAGO, 2003.

JINGLE DRESS DANCERS DURING AN INTERTRIBAL, UNIVERSITY OF ILLINOIS AT CHICAGO, 1986.

WOMEN'S JINGLE DRESS DANCE

The Women's Jingle Dress Dance is named for the metal cone decorated dresses worn by the dancers. Jingle Dress Dancers are often called upon to dance for a sick community member and is considered a healing dance.

Traditionally, 365 cones, called jingles, are sewn onto the dress representing each day of the year and a prayer is put into each cone. Jingles are made from the tin lids of tobacco snuff cans. While dancing, these metal cones hit against one another creating a rich jingling sound. During the honor beats of a song, the Jingle Dress Dancer uses her fan to spread the prayers into the four directions, releasing the prayers from the 'dancing cones', or jingles.

ELIZABETH BEGAY, UNIVERSITY OF ILLINOIS AT CHICAGO, 2003.

There are numerous stories of the origin of the Jingle Dress. According to one of them, the Jingle Dress came about as a result of a dream from an Ojibwe spiritual leader. In his dream, he was told that four dresses of this kind were to be made and worn at a special gathering. He was also taught the songs and particular dance steps. The dancers do not turn completely around while dancing.

JINGLE DRESS DANCERS, UNIVERSITY OF ILLINOIS AT CHICAGO, 2003.

SARAH GARVIN, NAES COLLEGE POWWOW, MATHER PARK, 2002.

Hodazha-Maniwinga Pidgeon (left), Kanikisa Corbin (center back) and Kanowan Kayotawape (right), Northeastern Illinois University, 2002.

Norma Robertson (foreground), Pam Auxier (left) Evanston, 2002.

George Martin, Head Veteran Followed by Veterans Carrying Eagle Staffs and Flags, University of Illinois at Chicago, 2003.

Ron Jourdan, Head Veteran, University of Illinois at Chicago, 2001.

Grand Entry, University of Illinois at Chicago, 2001.

Visiting Royalty, Grand Entry, University of Illinois at Chicago, 2003.

"Tha Tribe" Singers, Northeastern Illinois University, 2002.

Ronnie Preston, Grass Dancer, University of Illinois at Chicago, 2000.

Fancy Dancer Wayne Silas Jr. (left), and Roland Barker (right), NAES College Annual Powwow, Mather Park, 2001.

Grass Dancer, University of Illinois at Chicago, 2003.

KEVIN LOCKE, HOOP DANCER UNIVERSITY OF ILLINOIS AT CHICAGO, 2003.

HOOP DANCE
The Hoop Dance represents the sacred circle of life. The person that performs this dance is the center of that scared circle. In order for one to attain the ability to perform the dance, one must receive it through a vision or through a dream that must be interpreted through a Holy Man.

The Hoop Dance is a symbolic representation of an animal or a winged relative in honor of their natural essence.

Gunya Cornelius, Amber Cleveland, Terrylee Hindsley, and Lynsay Tomow, Fancy Shawl Dancers, Grand Entry, Northeastern Illinois University, 2002.

Jingle Dress Dancers, Grand Entry, University of Illinois at Chicago, 1996.

Junior Miss Indian Chicago Sylvia Dames and Shann Maupin, University of Illinois at Chicago, 1998.

Linsay Tomow (left) and Alicia Summers (right), Fancy Shawl Dancers, University of Illinois at Chicago, 2003.

Little Miss Indian Chicago Ashley Funmaker, American Indian Center Royalty, University of Illinois at Chicago, 2000.

Two-Step Dancers Valerie D'Ana and Neal Warrington, University of Illinois at Chicago, 2003.

FOOD VENDORS WAYNE SILAS, SR. AND JOHN DALL, NAES COLLEGE ANNUAL POWWOW, MATHER PARK, 2001.

Women's Fancy Shawl Dancer, Navy Pier Ballroom, 1986.

TERESA MAGNUSON, NORTHEASTERN ILLINOIS UNIVERSITY, 2002.

WOMEN'S FANCY SHAWL DANCE

The Women's Fancy Shawl Dance is considered to be a relatively new style of dancing that originated when women started making shawls in the early 1900s to replace the blanket and buffalo robes they would wear in public. This energetic and graceful dance originally afforded young women an opportunity to showcase their new shawls. Another story tells that the young ladies and their shawls represent the transition from a cocoon to a beautiful butterfly. Beadwork and accessories match the multi-fringed shawls. Fancy footwork, the main component of the dance, is performed to the changing beat of the Drum, creating a splendor of spinning colors and elaborate movements.

FANCY SHAWL DANCER, 1983.

Josee Starr, NAES College Annual Powwow, Mather Park, 2002.

Jennifer O'Rourke, NAES College Annual Powwow, Mather Park, 2003.

AMERICAN INDIAN CENTER, c. 1984.

INTERTRIBAL

A common misrepresentation of powwow culture remains that it is exclusively a Native American activity. This could not be further from the truth. Powwow is a time of gathering for the purpose of diverse interaction and wholesome recreation with a Native essence. Throughout the duration of a powwow, intertribal dancing is offered giving the entire powwow community an opportunity to actively participate in the fourth circle. One does not need dance regalia to enter the circle. Intertribal dancing is a time for inclusive festivity. Dancers move "sunwise" (clockwise), maintaining the fourth circle. As the emcee exclaims, "Let's do what you came here to do, let's powwow! Everybody dance!"

Barbara Bearskin (center) and Cyndee Starr (right), American Indian Center, 1984.

Cleo White (center) and Dennis White (right), Intertribal Dance, University of Illinois at Chicago, 2003.

MIKAYLA TEHYA, RIVER FOREST, 2001.

TINY TOTS
People of all ages participate in powwows, even the youngest of children.

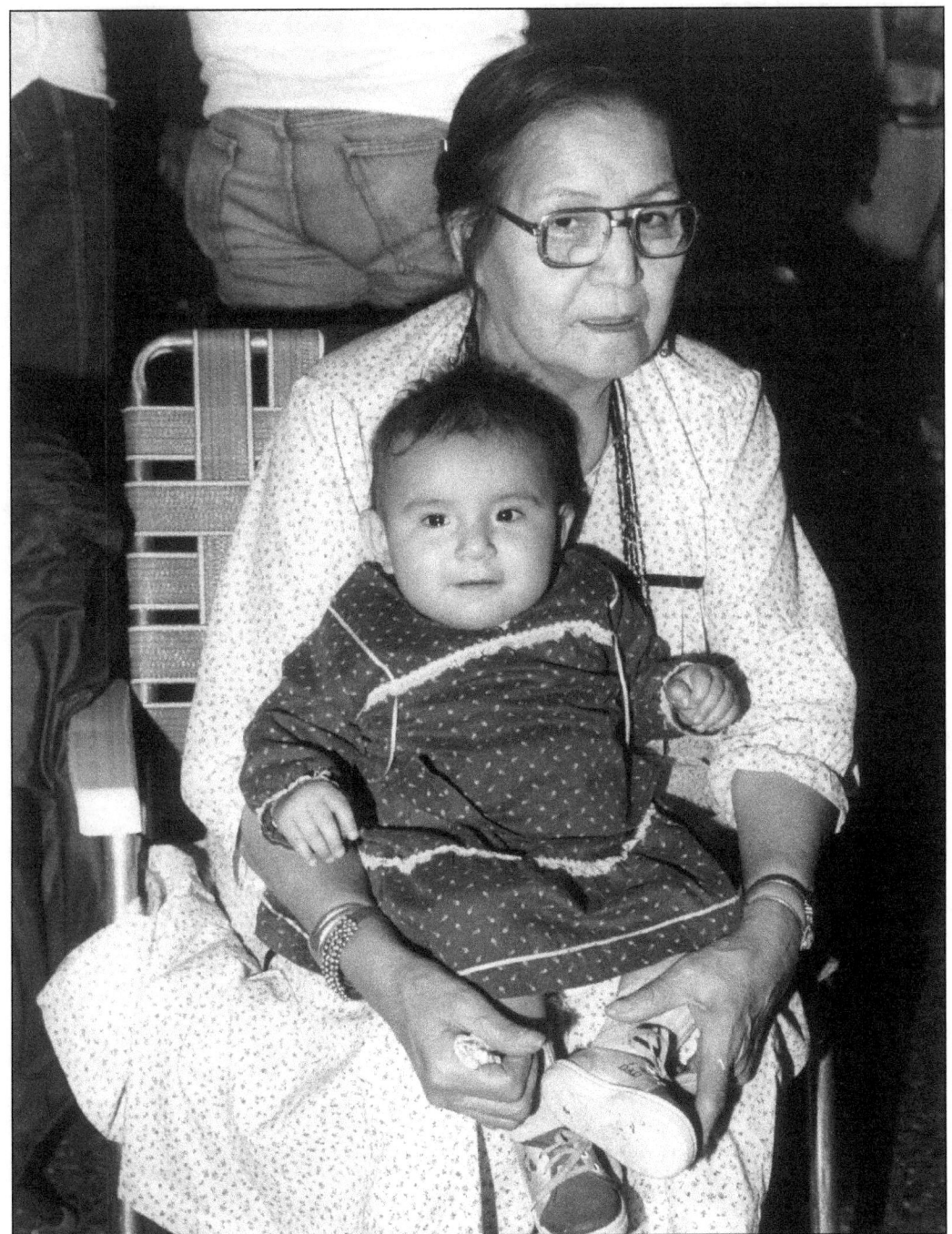

ROSELLA MALLORY HOLDING DENISE LOGAN, CHICAGO AVENUE ARMORY, 1978.

ELDERS AND COMMUNITY MEMBERS
The older generation holds a revered place within the American Indian community. Elders are the keepers of tradition and insure that Native arts and knowledge are passed from one generation to the next.

SUSAN POWER, MELVIN GREY OWL, AND MARGARET CHASE, NORTHEASTERN ILLINOIS UNIVERSITY, 2002.

ROBERT WAPAHI, UNIVERSITY OF ILLINOIS AT CHICAGO, 2003.

MAVIS NECONISH WITH AIC ROYALTY MISS INDIAN CHICAGO ANGELICA MAHKIMETAS AND JUNIOR MISS INDIAN CHICAGO ARISSA YOLANDA ST. GERMAINE, UNIVERSITY OF ILLINOIS AT CHICAGO, 2003.

MOTHERS AND DAUGHTERS: SUSAN POWER, JR. AND SUSAN POWER (BACKGROUND), ROSE MANEY AND ILONA MANEY (FOREGROUND), UNIVERSITY OF ILLINOIS AT CHICAGO, 2001.

LEFT TO RIGHT: VALENTINA KOJOVIC, CLOVIA MALATARE (IN TRADITIONAL WOMEN'S REGALIA), DOLORES AND JOE ZAWADZKI, UNIVERSITY OF ILLINOIS AT CHICAGO, 2003.

ROBYN ISAAC, UNIVERSITY OF ILLINOIS AT CHICAGO, 2003.

SUSAN POWER AND MARY
GREENDEER, UNIVERSITY OF
ILLINOIS AT CHICAGO, 2003.

NORMA BEARSKIN AND SYLVIA
BATTISTE KING, NAVY PIER
BALLROOM, 1983.

YOUTH TAKING A BREAK FROM DANCING, 1984.

JOSEPH PODLASEK, CORINNE FLOOD, AND RON KELTY, NAES COLLEGE ANNUAL POWWOW, MATHER PARK, 2003.

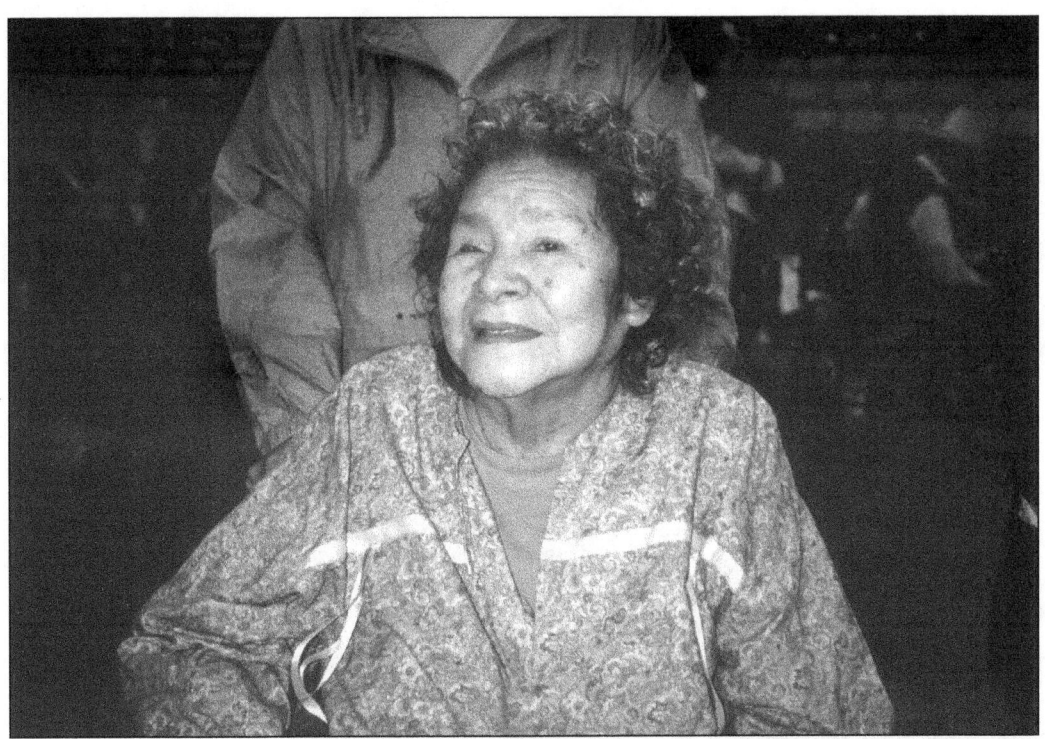

Margaret Redcloud, University of Illinois at Chicago, 2001.

Vincent Catches, University of Illinois at Chicago, 2001.

Corinne Flood, University of Illinois at Chicago, 2001.

William Flood, University of Illinois at Chicago, 2001.

TRADITIONAL WOMEN DANCERS IN FOREGROUND, 1984.

RON BOWAN, RON JOURDAN, FRANK FIGUEROA, AND CHARLES BELISLE, UNIVERSITY OF ILLINOIS AT CHICAGO.

FANCY DANCERS, NAVY PIER BALLROOM, 1984.

TINY TOT, NAVY PIER BALLROOM, 1984.

Six
SPECIALS AND VENDORS

The Give-Away is an integral part of a powwow as it represents the generous nature of Native peoples. Give-Aways allow an individual(s) to mark an important occasion, for example, being a Head Dancer or dancing in the circle for the first time. Giving gifts is a way of honoring certain individuals or groups among Indian people. Here the gesture is far more important than the value of the gift; it is an honor both to receive and to give gifts.

Specials are unique in their own right. Specials are a series of unique activities that are performed within the dance arena—the fourth circle. Specials take various forms and include many types and themes. Specials include: memorials through song and dance; acknowledgements for individual or group accomplishments; Hand Drum contests and exhibition dances including:

THE TWO STEP
The Two Step is one of a few dances where men and women dance as partners. Women choose their partners. Couples, holding hands, step off with the left foot and continue, dragging the right foot up in time to Grandfather's heartbeat. If a man refuses an invitation to dance, he has to "pay" (money or craft item) to the asker.

FISH DANCE
Performed by the men and boys, it is an interpretation of the life of a fish. The dance requires agility on the part of participants as they imitate the movement of the inhabitants of lakes and streams.

SNAKE DANCE
A social dance which is an interpretation of the life cycle of the snake. Dancers follow each other in a single line, moving in and out in a snake-like manner. The colorful line of dancers weave throughout the arena and curls into a tight circle as the snake goes to sleep. Then the dancers unwind to depict the awakening of the snake, and the "shedding of the skin."

SWAN DANCE
A Woodland dance which imitates the birds in flight. The leader is followed by dancers who will move into a "V" formation at the change in the drumbeat. Women and girls perform this elegant dance.

ROUND DANCE
In the Round Dance, dancers move in rows of circles clockwise around the drum in a side-step, with the faster moving line in the middle close to the drum and the slower toward the outside. The entire line moves as one body, each in harmony with the rhythm of the drum.

ARISSA YOLANDA ST. GERMAINE GIVEAWAY, UNIVERSITY OF ILLINOIS AT CHICAGO, 2003.

ANGELICA MAHKIMETAS GIVEAWAY, UNIVERSITY OF ILLINOIS AT CHICAGO, 2003.

CHILDREN RECEIVE CANDY AS PART OF 'GIVEAWAY', UNIVERSITY OF ILLINOIS AT CHICAGO, 2003.

NATIVE YOUTH PICKING UP CANDY AT 'GIVEAWAY', UNIVERSITY OF ILLINOIS AT CHICAGO, 2003.

Adrian Klein Jr (Cubby) at his First Dance with Parents, Adrian Klein and Nizhoni Hodge, University of Illinois at Chicago, 2003.

Tristan Podlasek, First Dance Giveaway, University of Illinois at Chicago, 2003.

SPECIAL HAND-DRUM COMPETITION, UNIVERSITY OF ILLINOIS AT CHICAGO, 2003.

JOHN SWIFTBIRD (CENTER), HAND-DRUM COMPETITION, UNIVERSITY OF ILLINOIS AT CHICAGO, 2003.

HELEN HARDEN AND SONNY WATERS, TWO STEP DANCE, AMERICAN INDIAN FESTIVAL AT THE FIELD MUSEUM, 1968.

MICHELLE BERGLOFF AND ROGER CRABB, TWO STEP DANCE, UNIVERSITY OF ILLINOIS AT CHICAGO, 2003.

Two Step Dance, University of Illinois at Chicago, 2003.

Joseph Podlasek, U.S. Congresswoman Jan Schakowsky, and Ron Kelty, Millennium Park, 2003.

General Federation of Women Clubs Representatives with Joseph Podlasek (right) and Ron Kelty, University of Illinois at Chicago, 2003.

Valerie Wilson (center) at AIC Information Table, University of Illinois at Chicago, 2003.

Artists and Vendors

Powwow provides a magnificent platform for first-voice Native artistic expression, as artists from around the country display their work in a colorful and vibrant marketplace. Artists, vendors, and community organizations come together in a shared space where visitors interact with the Native community. In all regards, powwow is an extended showcase of the Native artist/teacher/storyteller who offers traditional aspects of culture through an indigenous lens. Collectively, the following images encompass art and stories from Indian Country. These artists provide elaborate and original works, indicative of various media (e.g. beadwork, silversmithing, Drum making, ceramics, leather and feather work, etc.). Thus, multiculturalism is expressed. The contemporary powwow provides opportunities to share daily cultural practice paramount to our Native families, community, and friends.

Tom and Vivian Mason Family, c. 1979.

Dan Battiste, Arts and Craft Vendor, Navy Pier, 1979.

MARGUERITE (MIKIE) BOWAN, NORTHEASTERN ILLINOIS UNIVERSITY, 2002.

MARY GREENDEER (LEFT), LORRAINE DEON, AND ANSEL DEON, NORTHEASTERN ILLINOIS UNIVERSITY, 2002.

VENDOR AT POWWOW, UNIVERSITY OF ILLINOIS AT CHICAGO, 2003.

JOE SPENCER, NORTHEASTERN ILLINOIS UNIVERSITY, 2002.

Dorothy Antonio, University of Illinois at Chicago, 2003.

Vendors at Powwow, Dave Farnham (left), Northeastern Illinois University, 2002.

NICK CYWINK AND KIM MOODIE, UNIVERSITY OF ILLINOIS AT CHICAGO, 2003.

TRIBAL INFORMATION BOOTH, NORTHEASTERN ILLINOIS UNIVERSITY, 2003.

Olivia Kelty (left), Annette Kelty (center), and Ron Bowan (left), Northeastern Illinois University, 2002.

Helen Harden, Northeastern Illinois University, 2003.

Overview of Marketplace, Northeastern Illinois University, 2002.

Seven
NEXT GENERATION

Powwows give our community important chances to prosper and strengthen the cultural and social traditions that are so important to the sustenance of our people. Powwows create a critical vehicle for transmitting those traditions to our younger generation.

TINY TOT (FOREGROUND), AMERICAN INDIAN CENTER POWWOW, c. 1960s.

MICHELLE KLEIN (LEFT), CASEY HINDSLEY, GINA HINDSLEY, AND FRIEND, NAVY PIER, 1983.

JENNIFER WHITE (CENTER) AND
GRETCHEN STROUSE (RIGHT),
CHICAGO AVENUE ARMORY, 1975.

Traditional Dancer Taking a Break, AIC Powwow.

Davis Wounded Eye and Winfield Redcloud Wounded Eye, University of Illinois at Chicago, 2003.

Frank and Antonio Figueroa, University of Illinois at Chicago, 2003.

Lyle and Ansel Deon, Northeastern Illinois University, 2002.

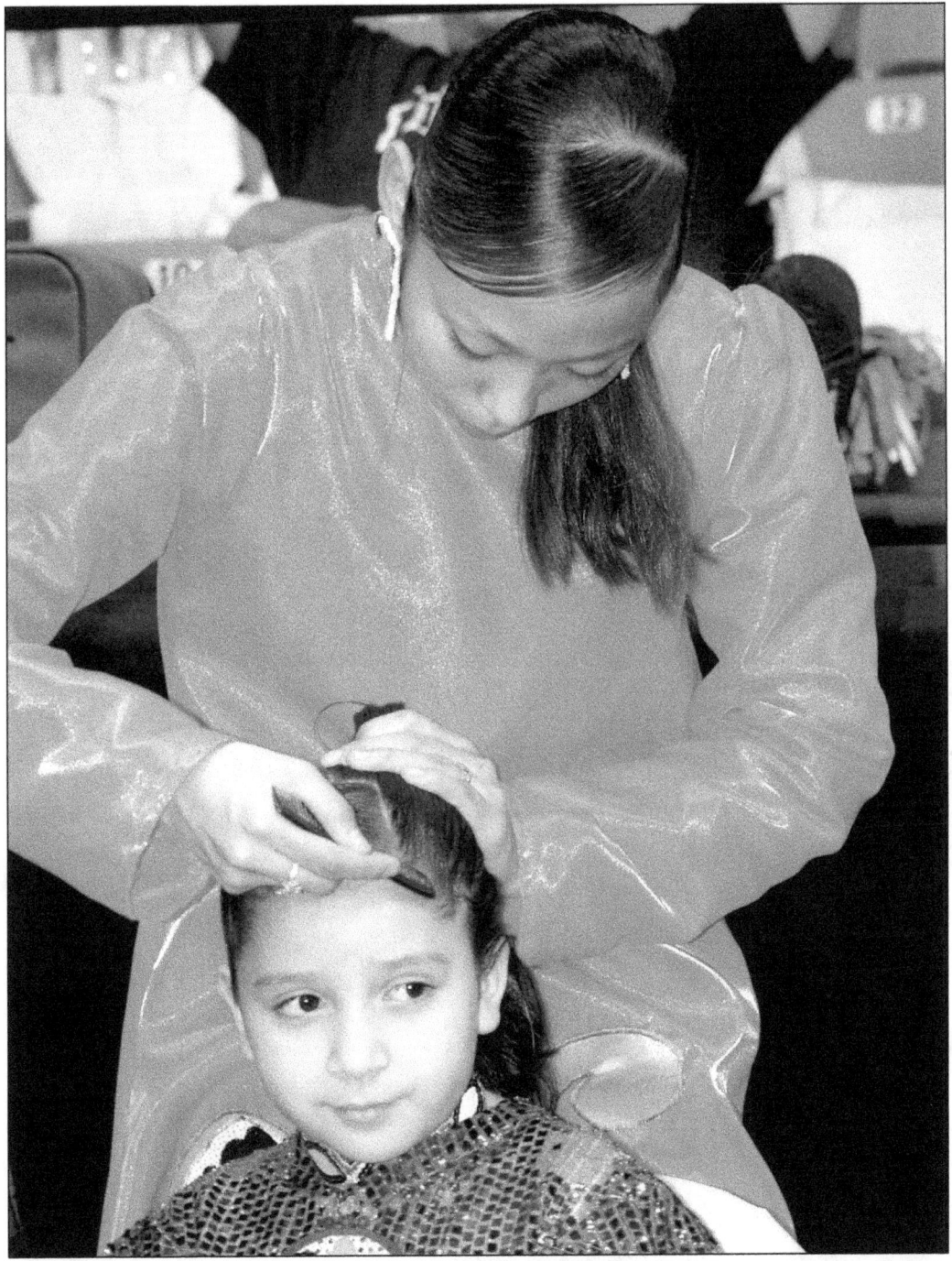

TASHELLAH KING AND HODAZHA-MANIWINGA PIDGEON, UNIVERSITY OF ILLINOIS AT CHICAGO, 2003.

YOUTH AT POWWOW, UNIVERSITY OF ILLINOIS AT CHICAGO, 2003.

CHRISTINE REDCLOUD AND WINFIELD REDCLOUD WOUNDED EYE, MILLENNIUM PARK, 2003.

Adrian Klein Jr. (Cubby), University of Illinois at Chicago, 2003.

Calvin Hill and Son, University of Illinois at Chicago, 2003.

Ashley Funmaker (left) and Hodazha-Maniwinga Pidgeon (right), University of Illinois at Chicago, 1999.

Young Dancers, AIC Powwow, 1984.

YOUNG GIRL AT POWWOW, AIC POWWOW, 1984.

TRISTAN AND STEVEN PODLASEK,
UNIVERSITY OF ILLINOIS AT
CHICAGO, 2001.

DARYL JACK, FANCY DANCER, UNIVERSITY OF ILLINOIS AT CHICAGO, 2003.

KYLE FUNMAKER, UNIVERSITY OF ILLINOIS AT CHICAGO, 2003.

Eight
50 YEARS OF POWWOW
THE EXHIBITION OF STORYTELLING

"50 Years of Powwow" is a triumphant visual arts exhibition commemorating 50 years of community and cultural celebration.

As a result, the exhibition accomplishes placement of Native Americans into the 21st century, laying to rest the myth of dependency and replacing it with a message of self-determination and cultural pride.

"50 Years of Powwow" portrays a retrospective of Chicago powwows. This collection of photographs fuses contemporary media with the ancient practice of storytelling. For centuries, Native American storytelling has been an oral tradition, establishing teachings from generation to generation. "50 Years of Powwow" is an act of celebration and a re-appropriation of image as we combat years of misrepresentation by mass media and pop culture. "50 Years of Powwow" is aimed at enhancing an unwritten culture, to provide first-voice insight into intertribal-urban-Native American customs.

The themes produced by "50 Years of Powwow" covers issues relating to the role of family, the role of the veteran as the protector, the survival of language through the oral tradition (song), Chicago Native American Intertribal history, and personal stories that reflect pride, dignity, patriotism, resistance, and the evolution and consequences of a community of displaced people.

Our goals are both to explore traditionalism—targeting the question of fusing traditions into contemporary Western ideology and methodology—and provide understanding of why Native Americans do what they do. Retaining traditional practices in urban centers has been difficult; living in two worlds presents a unique lifestyle and environment.

"50 Years of Powwow" provides a platform for dialogue and understanding of contemporary Native American life, from historical tragedies and displacement to how these occurrences affect Native People, the loss and/or evolution of traditional practices, and Native identity today.

"50 Years of Powwow" is an opportunity to share in the oldest form of social gathering in North America.

Inez Dennison, Irene Bedard, Clifford Blackbird, Ron Kelty, Susan Power, and Josephine Fox, New Year's Eve Celebration, American Indian Center of Chicago, 2002.

AMERICAN INDIAN CENTER OF CHICAGO
In recognition of the 50th Anniversary of the American Indian Center of Chicago, on New Year's Eve, December 31, 2002, the "50 Years of Powwow" exhibition opened at the American Indian Center. These photographs highlight 50 years of Chicago Powwows.

IRENE BEDARD AND DENI PERFORM AT NEW YEAR'S EVE CELEBRATION, AMERICAN INDIAN CENTER OF CHICAGO, 2003.

CHRISTINA RIFE (LEFT) HOLDING HER DAUGHTER, AGIINA PODLASEK, WITH ERIN MCNAMARA, NEW YEAR'S EVE CELEBRATION, AMERICAN INDIAN CENTER OF CHICAGO, 2003.

CRICKETTHILL SINGERS PERFORMING AT THE CHICAGO HISTORICAL SOCIETY "50 YEARS OF POWWOW" OPENING, FEBRUARY 8, 2003,

CHICAGO HISTORICAL SOCIETY
The "50 Years of Powwow" exhibition opened on Saturday, February 8, 2003, at the Chicago Historical Society. The Cricketthill Singers performed at the opening and there was a presentation by Joseph Podlasek, executive director of the American Indian Center.

JOE PODLASEK TALKING TO A GROUP AT THE OPENING, 2003.

JOE PODLASEK (LEFT), WARREN PERLSTEIN, NORA LLOYD, JANE STEVENS, AND DAVID SPENCER, EXHIBITION ORGANIZERS AT THE CHICAGO HISTORICAL SOCIETY OPENING ON SATURDAY, FEBRUARY 8, 2003.

The Field Museum

The Field Museum presented the "50 Years of Powwow" exhibition from July 2003–January 18, 2004 in the Marae Gallery. At the opening, there were community dancers and the Cricketthill Singers.

Dance and Drum Presentation at The Field Museum Opening Reception, July 2003.

Raeanne Hidalgo, Jingle Dress Dancer, 2003.

The Field Museum Installation of "50 Years of Powwow" Exhibition, July 2003.

R.J. Smith, Traditional Dancer, The Field Museum, July 2003.

Miss Indian Chicago Angelica Mahkimetas (left), and Shki Bmaadzi Drum with Christine Redcloud (right) at Opening Reception, September 12, 2003.

Illinois State Museum Chicago Gallery

On September 12, 2003, the Illinois State Museum Chicago Gallery's exhibition opened. R.J. Smith did a presentation and the Shki Bmaadzi Drum performed. The gallery is located in the James R. Thompson Center in Chicago. The exhibition ran from September 12 to November 7, 2003.

Pat Xerikos and Joe Podlasek (foreground), Kent Smith, Director of Art, ISM (background), September 2003.

Video Projection "Let's Powwow" by Nancy Bechtol, September 2003.

DAVID SPENCER SPOKE TO A GROUP AT THE DICKSON MOUNDS GALLERY RECEPTION, JANUARY 11, 2004.

ILLINOIS STATE MUSEUM DICKSON MOUNDS
On January 11, 2004, the "50 Years of Powwow" exhibition opened at Dickson Mounds in Central Illinois. David Spencer and Ansel Deon did a presentation along with the Cricketthill Singers. The exhibition ran through April 10, 2004.

VISITORS VIEW VIDEO AT DICKSON MOUNDS GALLERY, JANUARY 2004.

VIEW OF GALLERY INSTALLATION, DICKSON MOUNDS, JANUARY 2004.

OPENING RECEPTION, SPURLOCK MUSEUM, UNIVERSITY OF ILLINOIS, CHAMPAIGN-URBANA, FEBRUARY 22, 2004.

SPURLOCK MUSEUM, UNIVERSITY OF ILLINOIS, CHAMPAIGN-URBANA
From January 27 to June 26, 2004, the "50 Years of Powwow" exhibition was presented at the Spurlock Museum at the University of Illinois, Champaign-Urbana. On Sunday, February 22, 2004, there was a reception and performance by American Indian dancers and Cricketthill Singers.

VIEW OF GALLERY EXHIBITION, SPURLOCK MUSEUM, UNIVERSITY OF ILLINOIS, CHAMPAIGN-URBANA, FEBRUARY 2004.

GALLERY VIEW, SPURLOCK MUSEUM, UNIVERSITY OF ILLINOIS, CHAMPAIGN-URBANA.

DAVID SPENCER AND KELLY GILBRETH PROMOTING THE "50 YEARS OF POWWOW" EXHIBITION AND THE FIRST NATIONS FILM FESTIVAL, UNIVERSITY OF ILLINOIS AT CHICAGO, 2003.

AMERICAN INDIAN CENTER'S 50TH ANNUAL POWWOW
The American Indian Center of Chicago's 50th Annual Powwow was held November 14, 15, and 16, 2003 at the University of Illinois at Chicago Pavilion. A selection of photographs from the "50 Years of Powwow" exhibition was on display at the powwow.

Ron Kelty, AIC Board Chairman, University of Illinois at Chicago, 2003.

Joe Podlasek (left), Cook County Treasurer Maria Pappas, and Ron Kelty, University of Illinois at Chicago, 2003.

THE NEWBERRY LIBRARY'S D'ARCY MCNICKLE CENTER FOR AMERICAN INDIAN HISTORY

On behalf of The Newberry Library's D'Arcy McNickle Center for American Indian History, I am honored to contribute a few sentences to this important visual record of 50 years of powwow, sponsored by the American Indian Center of Chicago. For half a century, the AIC has stood at the center of the American Indian community in Chicago, and as these photographs demonstrate, a vibrant community it is indeed.

Photographs in the Newberry Collection originated in a two year pilot oral history project completed in 1984. Built around interviews with members of the Chicago Indian community, the Chicago Indian Photography project began as an effort to preserve a visual record of this city's native community, and featured the work of photographers Dan Battiste, Ben Bearskin, Orlando Cabanban, Joe Kazumura, F. Peter Weil, and Leroy Wesaw. Their photos formed the core of "Seeing Indian in Chicago," an exhibit which promoted community pride at the same time that it reminded non-Indians of the long history of native people in Chicago. Running from July 22-September 21, 1985, this exhibit was organized by Dorene Wiese, then assistant to the vice president of Truman College, and David R. Miller, formerly associate director of the McNickle Center, but really was a collaborative venture, bringing together community members and scholars all in common cause.

Because many of these photographs are housed at The Newberry Library, they also illuminate the decades-long connections between Chicago's American Indian community and McNickle Center staff. For three decades, the McNickle Center has worked to foster respectful relations between academic scholars who use the Library's collections, and native peoples, locally, regionally, and nationally. It is our belief that responsible scholarship must not be conducted in a vacuum, and that all of us, academics and community scholars, non-Indian students and native historians, can and should learn from one another. Indeed, we must communicate, and share.

To this end, the Library and the AIC have worked together in a number of ways, from collaboration on public events like "Winter, a Time of Telling," to annual research conferences that bring nationally-renowned scholars to Chicago. A portion of this project was supported by a short-term fellowship made possible by the Rockefeller Foundation. And for that, we are grateful to that institution, and to Jane Stevens who made wonderful use of the support, and enlightened us all to the rich collections in our midst.

So this volume should be seen firstly as a visual record of a vibrant and exciting community, its people, and activities. But I also like to think of it as a record of productive collaboration, sets of relationships that enrich us all.

–Brian Hosmer, Director
D'Arcy McNickle Center for American Indian History

SERENA YELLOWBANK, STEVE KING, AND BARBARA WHITEHEAD, NAVY PIER BALLROOM, c. 1983.

STEVE KING AND SARAH KEAHNA, AMERICAN INDIAN CENTER OF CHICAGO, c. 1983.

ALL TRIBES AMERICAN INDIAN CENTER, 1953. (Photograph donated to the American Indian Center by the Maney Family in 2003.)

AIC COMMUNITY MEMBERS, MILLENNIUM PARK, 2003.

American Indian Center of Chicago

AIC History

Founded in 1953, the American Indian Center (AIC) is the oldest urban Indian organization in the country. According to the 2000 U.S. Census, there are approximately 73,000 Native Americans in Illinois, including 30,000 residing in metropolitan Chicago, making it the third largest urban-Native community in the United States. Representing over 100 tribes, the AIC has entered its 50th year as a visible symbol of Chicago's diverse multi-tribal community in search of common social and cultural ground.

AIC is committed to promoting the well-being, education, and economic development of this Native American community, while simultaneously completing our mission to "... create bonds of understanding and communication..." by advancing ideals of tolerance and diversity. AIC and its programs lay to rest the myth of dependency and justly represent Native Americans as integral participants in modern society. Inclusive programs and services provided by the AIC address both short-term basic needs and long-term training and support. There are four important focus areas: cultural activities, social services, health, and education. The AIC provides such programs as: (cultural activities) powwows and special events such as presentations of music, dance, film, art, story-telling, and teen talking circles; (social services) Hot Meals program, food pantry and clothing donations; (health) Health and Wellness Center and the Daughters of Tradition; (education) free computer classes, the Positive Paths tutoring and mentoring program, and the School Tour Program which reaches Chicago's diverse student and teacher population.

Through the years, the AIC has helped thousands of American Indians from all across the country transition successfully into urban life. AIC has been the principal cultural resource for Indian Chicago. While no tribal reservations exist in Illinois, the very existence of the AIC fills a void in a region where Native communities continue to be overlooked and underserved.

Across the country, in reservations and urban centers, Native American people have a wealth of traditional practices. The AIC provides space to celebrate and foster a continuum of this irreplaceable culture.

AIC has begun to receive recognition for its unique work. Recently, the Smithsonian Institution selected the AIC to create and implement an exhibit about the urban Native experience for the new National Museum of the American Indian. The AIC was the only urban Indian organization, from the Western Hemisphere, to be selected for this honor. The inaugural exhibit entitled "Our Lives" will open in Washington D.C. in 2004.

As visitors to the AIC learn about Native history, contemporary culture, identity and cultural celebrations, they become aware of the Native American historical contribution to the cultural fabric of the City of Chicago and the State of Illinois.